HOW TO LIVE LIKE
A STONE AGE
HUNTER

By Anita Ganeri

Illustrated by Mariano Epelbaum

HUNGRY
TOMATO™

Contents

Stone Age Hunter

You've travelled back around 15,000 years to Europe during the Palaeolithic (Old Stone Age). A **clan** of **hunter-gatherers** is getting ready to go on a mammoth hunt. Food has been hard to come by, and everyone's hungry. The meat from a mammoth will keep them going for weeks...

My name's Dar and my clan's made up of my family: my Mum, Dad, sister, aunts, uncles, cousins and Grandad. We get on fine, most of the time. Dad told me about the mammoth hunt last night, it's the most exciting news EVER. I've been daydreaming about mammoths since I was a kid but I've never actually seen one.

If you want to survive in the Stone Age, you need to be tough. The weather can be very cold or very warm, there's not much food to eat and there are no mod cons like electricity. Think you've got what it takes?

People in the Stone Age were hunter-gatherers. They hunted animals, such as mammoths, for their meat and skins, caught fish and collected shellfish, berries, roots, fruits and nuts.

Why the 'Stone' Age?

You've ended up in **prehistoric** Europe at the time of the Stone Age. It got its name because, at that time, people were making their tools from stone. The Stone Age began around 2.5 million years ago and ended between 6,000 and 2,500 BC. It was divided into three parts:

1 Palaeolithic (Old Stone Age)

2 Mesolithic (Middle Stone Age)

3 Neolithic (New Stone Age)

Human History

While everyone's busy getting ready for the hunt, my Grandad's been giving me a quick history lesson. Grandad's great but I hope it's not going to take too long, I've got some fishing hooks I want to finish. Grandad says we belong to a group of human beings called **Homo sapiens**, who originally came from Africa. Wonder if it's warmer there?

| 2.5 m–300,000 years ago | 300,000–40,000 years ago | 40,000–10,000 years ago |
| **Lower Palaeolithic** | **Middle Palaeolithic** | **Upper Palaeolithic** |

Early humans make the first simple tools, such as hand axes, out of stone. (The oldest known stone tools are to be found in Africa.)

Homo sapiens begin to move out of Africa and spread to other parts of the world. They start wearing clothes.

People begin stitching clothes and painting cave walls. Some settle in permanent shelters and huts; many remain **nomadic.**

Neanderthals

Another group of early humans were the Neanderthals. They got their name from the place in Germany where lots of their fossils were found. Neanderthals were quite short and stocky, which helped them to cope with the cold. They first appeared around 400,000 years ago, but died out around 30,000 years ago. No one really knows why.

10,000 years ago–5,000 BC
Mesolithic

The ice covering Europe begins to melt, bringing warmer weather. People **domesticate** sheep, cattle and dogs for the first time.

5,000 BC–2,500 BC
Neolithic

People gradually tend to settle in one place and farm crops and animals for food. Writing is invented in Sumer, marking the start of history.

2,500 BC–800 BC
Bronze Age

For the first time ever, people make tools, weapons and jewellery from metals, such as copper and bronze (an alloy of copper and tin).

Camping Trip

Well, we packed up our old camp and set out early this morning, following the mammoth tracks we spotted a few days ago. It was quite exciting at first. But we've walked all day and we still haven't found the mammoth, so Dad says we're going to spend the next few nights in this cave. He's checking it out for cave bears – while I am getting ready to paint on some of the walls.

WARNING!

Don't stand too close to the fire as you will set your clothes alight!

Make your cave comfortable by lighting a fire and making your bed out of soft, dried grass and a blanket of fur or skin. You can also set up a windbreak made from wooden posts and skins, weighed down with large stones.

How to light a fire

A fire's vital for light, warmth, cooking, and scaring off wild animals. It's also a great place to sit and chat. But how do you go about lighting a fire?

1 Take a long stick and cut the end into a sharp point.

2 Carve a small hole in another, softer piece of wood.

3 Fit the stick in the hole, then twirl it quickly between the palms of your hands.

4 When the soft wood begins to smoulder, put some dry **tinder** on top. Then blow gently to make a flame.

If you want to keep your cave safe, get a guard dog (tame wolf). In return for a share of reindeer or mammoth meat, it'll protect you from hungry hyenas and other predators.

cave Art

Next morning, Dad and some of the men went to look for more mammoth signs (tracks and poo). My Uncle Gam stayed behind. He told me to grab a lighted torch and follow him into the cave. We went deeper and deeper, and it got darker and darker. Then, all of a sudden, I spotted reindeers and other animals… on the walls. Gam told me they'd been painted by hunters who'd used the cave last year to bring them good luck in the hunt.

Prehistoric artists made their paints from natural substances: red from **ochre** (clay) or hematite (a **mineral**); yellow from goethite (mineral) and black from manganese (mineral) or charcoal. For brushes, they used their fingers or burnt sticks.

How to hand tag

Leave your own mark on the cave wall with a couple of colourful hand tags. Here's what you need to do:

1 Pour some paint into a shallow bowl or shell.

2 Suck the paint up through a straw made from a hollow bone.

3 Put your hand flat on the wall as a stencil. Blow the paint around your hand.

Some of the greatest works of cave art are to be found in the Lascaux Caves in France. They were painted around 17,300 years ago and show animals, including horses, stags, bulls and even a rhinoceros.

Mammoth Shelter

While we were finding our way out again, Gam told me a story he'd heard about some mammoth hunters who live in a land far away in the east, in the direction of the sunrise. There's no stone to make tools from, and not much wood. But there are LOADS of mammoths, and the people build their huts from mammoth bones. How cool is that?

Dragging the bones to your site is a mammoth job in itself. You need around 25 mammoths to make one hut. One skull weighs around 100 kg; the bones in total weigh 20 tonnes, including about 36 tusks.

How to build a mammoth bone hut

Fed up with living in a cave? Want to build your own mammoth bone hut? Here's how:

1 Drag the mammoth bones to your site.

2 Make a ring of jawbones, one on top of the other, to form a solid base.

3 Use the huge, curved tusks to make an arch to support the roof and porch.

4 Lash other bones to the tusks for strength.

5 Cover the whole frame with hides.

You've built your hut and you've got one skull left over. What can you do with it? Why not put it in your porch to use as a drum? Decorate it with a flame-like pattern in red ochre. When you want to play it, use two long bones as drumsticks.

How to Make an Axe

Dad's back and says we're going hunting tomorrow, I CAN'T WAIT! So we're getting our weapons and tools ready. We make them from a type of stone called flint, which we get from the local **quarry**. Uncle Gam's the best flint-knapper in our clan (a flint-knapper's an expert at making tools). He's brilliant at making axe blades, knife blades, arrow heads… He says I'm a chip off the old block, whatever that means.

WARNING!

Don't worry if it takes a few tries to get your axe head right. Practice makes perfect. Just mind your fingers!

Flint is often white on the outside, and dark grey, green or brown inside. It is found in chalk or limestone rock. It's perfect for making tools and weapons because it splits into thin, sharp splinters.

Stone Age hunters also made spears from flint blades tied to long sticks, and harpoons for spearing fish. The harpoon points were horn from reindeer antler or ivory from mammoth tusks, which was extremely hard and strong.

How to make an axe

Here's Uncle Gam's tried-and-tested guide to making your own hand axe (without losing any of your fingers):

1 Choose a good, big piece of flint with no obvious cracks. (Tap it against another piece of flint. If it makes a nice ring, it's fine.)

2 Using another large stone as a hammer, chip away pieces to make the basic axe shape.

3 Create a sharp edge with a smaller stone or reindeer antler hammer.

4 Bind your axe head to a piece of wood, using cord made from animal gut, leather or hair. (You can also use this method to make a spear.)

How to Trap a Mammoth

The day of the mammoth hunt's finally here! At last. I've been practising hunting rabbits since I was five, but I've never been allowed to go after something this big before.

We followed the tracks and there it was! I've never seen anything so huge. Dad says the best way to trap a mammoth is to run as fast as you can after it and chase it into the nearest swamp, where it'll get stuck in the mud. That way, it won't be able to run away or attack us with its tusks. So, that's what we're going to do...

How to catch large animals

If you can't find a swamp, try this technique instead.
It works with all kinds of large animals, not just mammoths.

1 Pick your weapon carefully; a spear's best for this sort of thing.

2 Choose your animal: deer, bison, horse, camel or mammoth. They all taste great.

3 Find a high cliff and make a funnel shape on top of it with stones.

4 Herd the animal between the stones to guide it over the edge of the cliff.

5 Post one person at the bottom to make sure the animal's dead (but mind he doesn't get crushed).

6 Carve take-away chunks of the animal and carry them back to camp.

Keep an eye out for wolves – they'll scare off an animal before you've manoeuvred it anywhere near the cliff. To put a wolf out of action, dig a deep pit. Put a dead animal in the bottom as bait. Line the bottom of the trap with sharp sticks, then cover the top with leaves and branches. After that, it's a waiting game.

WARNING!

Don't go too near the edge of the cliff yourself, unless you've got a good head for heights.

19

Reindeer Rations

We did it! We killed the mammoth, even though it put up a good fight. We chased it into the swamp, then finished it off with our spears. Now we're dragging it back to camp. On the way, Dad spotted some reindeer and we've killed a couple of them, too. Dad said we might not get the chance to stock up on so much food for a while.

Mosquitoes can be a real pest, especially if you're camping near a stream. To avoid being bitten to death, rub some reindeer fat on your skin. You might not smell very nice but it should keep the irritating insects away.

How to use up (every bit of) a reindeer

Make the most of a reindeer catch, for food, tools and clothing – nothing needs to be wasted.

1 Antlers – for tools and weapons

2 Tongue, nose, eyeballs and brain – food rich in fat and protein

3 Bones – cracked open to get marrow which is high in fat; also boiled for fat and grease

4 Liver, kidneys and heart – also food rich in protein and fat

5 Skin – for making into clothes, bags, blankets and tents

After killing an animal, we eat some of the meat fresh, but also store some for winter when food is scarce. We freeze or dry it to stop it going off.

Battle of the clans

On the way back to camp, disaster struck. Hunters from another clan had been hiding, waiting in ambush for us. They'd seen us kill the mammoth and wanted to steal some of our meat. They must have been watching us for a long time.

A fight broke out, and it was chaos. Dad shouted to me to guard the mammoth while he and the others fought back. We seemed to be pushing them back but then I noticed Dad's cousin, Urg, lying on the ground…

How to throw a spear

Kowing how to use a spear-thrower is essential, because it can hurl a spear as far as 250 metres. Here's what you have to do:

1 Fit your spear into the groove at the back of the spear-thrower.

2 Hold the thrower in one hand, gripping the handle.

Spear-throwers are carved from wood or reindeer antlers. Some are decorated with carvings of animals. Pick something impressive, like a mammoth, for yours.

3 Swing your arm and throw...

4 ...the spear will fly out of the thrower.

cave Burial

What a dreadful day! We fought off the other clan (and saved our meat), but Urg was badly wounded. He had been hit by a spear and died last night. Because he was one of the leaders of our clan, we've brought his body to a secret cave where we will hold a special ceremony in his honour. We've painted his body with red ochre and laid his shell necklace and ivory staffs nearby. We've also left a mammoth skull.

Human bones found at Gough's Cave in Somerset, England, show a more sinister side to Stone Age burials. Some of the bones had been chewed by human teeth, and the skulls cut open and made into cups or bowls. It seems that the people of Gough's Cave may have been **cannibals**, but kept the skull as a way of honouring their dead.

A body found in Goat's Hole Cave, Paviland, Wales, may have been buried around 29,000 years ago. The body was called the 'Red Lady of Paviland' but was later found to be a man, possibly a clan chief.

Some Stone Age people were buried with precious possessions, such as carved deer antlers or teeth, shell or bead necklaces, pebbles and flint tools. Others were buried with nothing at all.

Stone Age Style

Back at camp, we're going to have a feast to remember Urg and celebrate a successful hunt. But first, I need some new clothes. Luckily, there's plenty of reindeer skin left over, so I'm having leggings, a tunic and new shoes – and probably a cap. The weather gets pretty chilly around here, so they'll need to be tough and warm. Then, we're going to sew some beads on the top and cap.

1

Stone Age people make necklaces and decorate their clothes with beads carved from mammoth ivory, shell, animal bones, teeth and jet. They drill holes in the beads with fine stone points. In some places, there are bead 'factories', making tens of thousands of beads.

How to make a Stone Age tunic

1 Scrape and then chew the skin to make it nice and soft.

2 Cut it into pieces to make the different parts of the tunic.

3 Punch holes in the skin with bone or ivory points.

4 Sew the pieces together, using a bone needle and gut or thin leather thread.

2

3

4

Final Feast

It's the night of the feast and everything is nearly ready. There's plenty to eat. Some of the meat is roasting over the fire, and we've got roots and berries and Dad has caught some fish. Everyone is gathering around the fire, and Uncle Gam's been telling stories of brave mammoth hunters and their daring deeds. It's going to be a great night, but it seems as if we'll soon be on the move again. The hunting here has been brilliant but it's nearly time to head south again for the winter.

A feast wouldn't really be a feast without music and dancing around the fire. Stone Age people played flutes and whistles, made from bird, bear, mammoth and deer bones.

Food was cooked on hot stones placed in the fire or on a spit made from wood. People also cooked meat by hanging up the carcass and wedging hot stones inside it.

There were no clay pots at this time. Containers were made from stone, leather, bark or reeds, possibly lined with clay to make them waterproof.

How to whistle

To make your own Stone Age whistle, all you need is a bone. There should be plenty of those lying around after the feast (if the dog hasn't got them).

1 Find a bone – the toe bone of a reindeer is ideal.

2 Scrape it clean, inside and out.

3 Use a pointed stone to bore a hole.

4 Blow across the hole to get a sound.

Even in the Stone Age a balanced diet was important, but it could be difficult to find enough veg in winter. Instead, you munched on half-digested **lichen** from a reindeer's stomach. Lichen is a reindeer's favourite food but it's tough for you to digest on your own.

Ten seriously cool Stone Age Facts

1 *Homo sapiens* are believed to have lived in Africa from around 200,000 years ago.

2 The oldest pieces of jewellery ever found are two tiny shell beads from Israel. They were made 100,000 years ago.

3 Experts think that people probably started talking more than 100,000 years ago. Some think that all languages come from one language spoken in Africa.

4 A skeleton found in France showed that Neanderthal people had the custom of burying their dead as long as 50,000 years ago.

5 The oldest-known musical instruments are two flutes, made from bird bone and mammoth ivory. They were found in southern Germany, and are over 40,000 years old.

6 In 1965, a mammoth-hut village was found at Mezhirich, Ukraine, dating back around 15,000 years.

7 A picture carved by the Mezhirich mammoth-hunters on a piece of mammoth ivory may be the world's oldest map.

8 The first farmers grew crops, such as wheat and rye, around 13,000 years ago in Syria.

9 During the Ice Age, some mammoths (and rhinoceroses) grew thick, woolly coats to keep them warm. On their undersides, their hair grew 1 metre long.

10 The bodies of thousands of mammoths have been found, perfectly preserved, in the frozen ground of Siberia, Russia.

Glossary

Cannibals

People who eat other people for food or as part of a ritual

Clan

A community of people with close links to each other

Domesticate

To tame a wild animal for farming or as a pet

Homo sapiens

The group of human beings to which we all belong

Hunter-gatherers

People who hunt animals and collect plants for food

Lichen

An edible mixture of a plant and a fungus

Mineral

A natural substance, found in rocks

Nomadic

People who move from place to place, in search of food and water

Ochre

A type of clay that can be yellow, orange, red or brown

Prehistoric

From a time in history before things were written down

Quarry

A place where rock and stone are dug up from the ground

Tinder

Wood, dried grass and other materials used for lighting fires

INDEX

The Author
Anita Ganeri is an award-winning author of educational children's books. She has written on a huge variety of subjects, from Vikings to viruses and from Romans to world religions. She was born in India but now lives in England with her family and pets.

The Artist
Mariano Epelbaum was born in Buenos Aires, Argentina. He grew up drawing and looking at small insects under the stones in the garden of his grandmother´s house. He has worked as an art director and character designer for many films in Argentina and Spain.